PRISCILLA'S PUZZLES: PHASE TWO

NEW

A WORD COLLECTOR WORKBOOK

Evelyn Dunbar Webb

BUMBLEMEYER PUBLICATIONS

CONCORD, VA

Bumblemeyer Publications
672 Spicer Road
Lynchburg, Virginia 24504

NOTICE TO EDUCATORS: Contact the publisher for special quantity discounts for bulk purchases. Book excerpts can also be created to fit specific educational needs. For details, please email the Education Coordinator, Bumblemeyer Publications, at bumblemeyerpub2017@outlook.com.

Book and Cover design by MotherWorld, an imprint of Bumblemeyer Publications
Cover illustration by Matt Tyree

First Bumblemeyer trade paperback edition: June 2017
Second edition: February 2024
ISBN: 978-1-9550380-7-2

This publication is part of a series of products and publications. For more information, please visit: https://www.bumblemeyer.com.

Printed in the United States of America

Contents

Introduction

Calling all logophiles and lexophiles!

In collaboration with author and illustrator Evelyn Dunbar Webb, Bumblemeyer Publications is proud to present an updated and expanded Language Arts workbook featuring Priscilla and her collection of words from her debut adventure, *The Word Collector*. Ideal for traditional classroom and home-school settings, *Priscilla's Puzzles* is designed to complement traditional textbooks with focused activities aligned with Virginia and Common Core Language Arts standards.

Join Priscilla and friends to solve new puzzles, complete worksheets, answer writing prompts, have fun with fill-in-the-blank stories, and write your own sentences. Then, develop your **own** word lists, and create and illustrate your **own** stories. And—the best part!—like Priscilla, **share** your words and stories with others.

Today you are you! That is truer than true! There is no one alive who is you-er than you!
Dr. Seuss

Quote Draw #1

Use the space below to draw a picture of yourself with your friends, your pet, your favorite toys, or your favorite things to do.

Word Search #1

The following words can be found in the diagram below, reading forward, backward, up, down, and diagonally. Find the words and circle them.

sweet	bake
rhinoceros	icecream
pig	ghost
quietly	cereal
mountain	cook
often	boil

```
Z X D V U W E N K S X F G N H I
U H C J V L U X D S I B S Q C K
H V O J F Y E Z V I B N F E B K
L H O X T B F D X R A Y C V U Q
S G K E W J U G R P K R Q W O U
O H W J D J P F U B E M S V O Y
R O Y M P X I K N A M G X G N O
E S W D L K Y N M H U C R J H Y
C T L L N U I E H I C F V R C L
O D C Q E A Q I O W V C S Y O T
N D X W T X Z N H G Z S A D Z E
I J F N F F E X I B I A Z Y I I
H N U V O E Q N D O F R A B O U
R O Z P V G O O G I S O Q Y T Q
M V V C D W C C E L A E R E C Q
S W E E T X J H L P I G M M C N
```

Scramble #1

Below is list of scramble words. Unscramble all the letters to reveal the words.

1. WYARFAA = _____

2. YDTSU = _____

3. AENLC = _____

4. OAEPSTOT = _____

5. DUNLSDYE = _____

6. NHBGCWIETI = _____

7. SYMLLE = _____

8. ISSEMEOMT = _____

Cryptogram #1

Each of these Cryptograms is a message in substitution code. THE SILLY DOG might become UJD WQPPZ BVN if U is substituted for T, J for H, D for E, etc. One way to break the code is to look for repeated letters. E, T, A, O, N, R, and I are the most often used letters. A single letter is usually A or I; OF, IS, and IT are common 2-letter words; try THE or AND for a 3-letter group.

The code is different for each Cryptogram. A Scratch Paper page is provided, and each puzzle includes three Hints to help you find the solution.

1. Wnf vsb isap sbwechbz aw oxhehbz.
   (V.U. Gpohu)   Hints: W = Y   S = A   B = N

2. Mn etdm etnzr pv ctnzbl. (Mddctdm
   Masldu)   Hints: E = G   T = R   N = E

3. Inmt tnhy gnv vbzw infptwadtht.
   (Ubyc Xbbgtc)   Hints: N = A   I = M   W = R

12

Scratch Paper

Noun Sort

Read the list of nouns in the Word Bank. Then write each word in the correct section below the list.

Remember: **Nouns** name people, places, and things.

Word Bank

bread	butcher	cashier	closet	mail carrier
house	librarian	sneakers	cloud	mountain
potatoes	school	store	thunder	rhinoceros
library	wizard	bicycle	teacher	grandparent
ostrich	aunt	daffodil	moat	doctor
hospital				jewelry

People	Places	Things
_____	_____	_____
_____	_____	_____
_____	_____	_____
_____	_____	_____
_____	_____	_____
_____	_____	_____
_____	_____	_____
_____	_____	_____
_____	_____	_____

Collective nouns are **nouns** that refer to a group of animals, people, things, etc. You have probably learned the term herd in reference to a group of cows and the term swarm for a group of bees. Herd and swarm are examples of collective nouns.

Below are two columns, the first with a list of various animals, birds, fish, insects, and reptiles and the second with a list of collective nouns. Draw a line from each of the creatures to their correct group term. The first creatures have been matched for you.

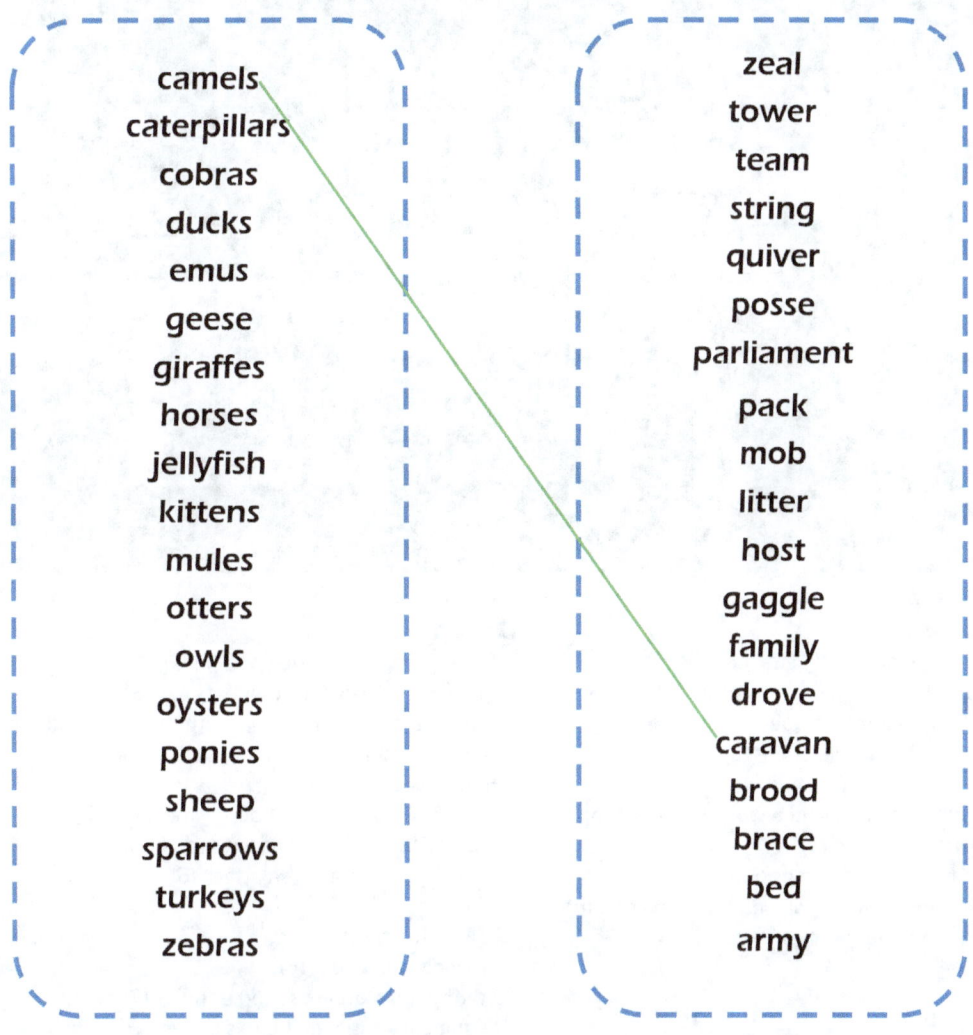

camels	zeal
caterpillars	tower
cobras	team
ducks	string
emus	quiver
geese	posse
giraffes	parliament
horses	pack
jellyfish	mob
kittens	litter
mules	host
otters	gaggle
owls	family
oysters	drove
ponies	caravan
sheep	brood
sparrows	brace
turkeys	bed
zebras	army

Crossword #1

Across

4 To force air through the nostrils (5)
8 To swoop down or leap and grab (6)
10 Breakfast food made from grain (6)
13 Clear to the eye or ear (5)
15 Stormy and untamed (4)
17 With elegance and beauty in movement (10)
18 Now and then (9)
19 Chunky; with bumps (5)
20 Feline mammal with whiskers and soft fur (3)
21 Without fear or hesitation (6)

Down

1 Awkward and without grace (6)
2 Mammal with hooves that eats hay (5)
3 Huge plant-eating mammal with thick skin and horns (10)
5 To make a loud, sharp cry like a dog (4)
6 Honored; satisfied (5)
7 To leap or hop up off a floor or the ground (4)
8 Mammal that snorts and likes mud (3)
9 To rush forward as in an attack (6)
11 Every time (6)
12 Sly or tricky (6)
14 Having a bad odor (6)
16 Without disturbing sound or noise (7)
22 Canine mammal that barks (3)

Cell Phone Mania #1

The messages below are in a number code based on how text messages are formed on a cell phone. Each number represents one of the letters shown on the picture of the phone to the right. You must decide which letter to use. A number is not necessarily the same letter each time.

1. 843 8463 47 259297 74448 86 36 9428
   47 74448. (627846 588437 5464, 57.)

2. 93 5669 9428 93 273 288 668 9428 93
   629 232663. (9455426 74253773273)

Sentence Mania #1

Priscilla needs your help to complete the sentences below. She has used some of the nouns, verbs, adverbs, and adjectives from the Word Bank, which are already crossed out, but the sentences still need at least two more words.

Read each sentence and the list of nouns, verbs, adverbs, and adjectives. Use the word clue to help you select the correct word to fill in each blank. Use each word only once and do not use any of the crossed-out words.

Word Bank

cereal	~~bread~~	potatoes	ice cream
cooked	~~bakes~~	boiled	~~was frozen~~
~~carefully~~	slowly	today	yesterday
~~lumpy~~	plain	~~mushy~~	sweet

1. Mrs. Thornblossom <u>carefully</u> _____ the <u>lumpy</u> _____.

2. The _____ <u>bread</u> _____ <u>bakes</u> in the oven.

3. Priscilla _____ <u>mushy</u> _____ for lunch _____.

4. The _____ _____ <u>was frozen</u> _____.

How Many Words #1

Using the letters in the word shown below, try to find as many 3-letter, 4-letter, 5-letter, 6-letter, and 7-letter words as you can. Write the words you discover in the spaces provided below. The first word has been provided for you.
NOTE: There are more possible word choices than spaces.

COLLYWOBBLES

COW

Keywords #1

To solve this puzzle, fill in the blanks below with the correct missing letter and then transfer the letter to the corresponding numbered square in the diagram below. Be careful! The puzzle is not as simple as it may first appear!

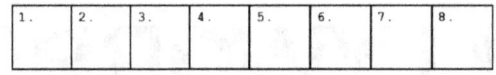

1. o _ t e n

2. c l _ a n

3. b _ r k

4. s _ o m p

5. m u s _ y

6. v _ r b

7. _ u m b l e

8. g e n t l _

Two In #1

Place two letters on the dashes to complete a word on the left and to begin another word on the right. For example, **SE** in between PLEA and VEN would completed **PLEASE** and begin **SEVEN**.

1. r i _ _ c r e t l y

2. a u _ _ d a y

3. b r e _ _ v e r b

4. r e _ _ j e c t i v e

5. r u m b _ _ g e n d a r y

Crypto Words #1

Each of these Crypto Words is written in substitution code. SILLY might become WQPPZ if W is substituted for S, Q for I, P for L, etc. When you have identified a word, use the known letters to decode the other words in the list. A Scratch Paper page is provided along with three Hints to help you.

Hints: L = I   Y = F   W = Y

1. QLUUFW = _____

2. YFRYYW = _____

3. YILBW = _____

4. HGKQ = _____

5. UXGZFW = _____

6. KYZXG = _____

7. HGXIVW = _____

8. UBIDXYRFFW = _____

Scratch Paper

Interweave #1

Rearrange and distribute the four letters accompanying each row so that you form a larger common word.

1. a c e d : __ __ j __ __ t i v e

2. s i n g : p h a __ t a __ m a __ o r __ c

3. c e r t : s __ __ __ e __ l y

4. a i d e : __ __ s __ p p __ a r

5. a c h e : l __ p r e __ __ __ u n

Story Tell #1

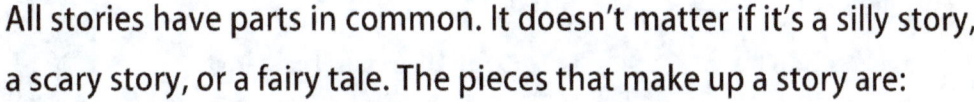

Storytelling is fun.

But storytelling can be difficult to start without help.

All stories have parts in common. It doesn't matter if it's a silly story, a scary story, or a fairy tale. The pieces that make up a story are:

- ✓ A main character (WHO)
- ✓ A problem (WHAT and WHY)
- ✓ A setting where the story happens (WHERE and WHEN)
- ✓ A solution (HOW)

Storytellers combine the WHO, WHAT, WHY, WHERE, WHEN, and HOW using nouns, verbs, adverbs, and adjectives.

The fairy tale on the next page is missing words. Read the story, and then fill in the blanks with the type of word described.

Be strange, be dreamy, be mysterious – but mostly, have fun!

Once upon a time, there was a _____ girl named Mollie.
(adjective)

Mollie lived with her _____ and _____
(noun)   (noun)

in a little _____ in the _____. One day,
(noun)   (noun)

while Mollie was at _____, a wicked _____
(noun)   (noun)

came to her _____ and cast a _____ to
(noun)   (noun)

make her parents _____. When Mollie came home from
(verb)

_____, she thought her _____ had gone
(noun)   (plural noun)

to the _____. But, _____ night _____
(noun)   (adverb)   (verb)

and she was still _____, Mollie became _____
(adjective)   (adjective)

She _____ the police and found out other _____
(verb)   (plural noun)

were also _____ _____ she was ready to _____,
(adjective)   (Adverb)   (verb)

Mollie decided she had to _____. She opened her grandma's
(verb)

old _____ and found the _____ her grandma used
(noun)   (noun)

when she was a _____. Then she stood _____ in the
(noun)   (adverb)

moonlight, and _____ the _____ word, "_____!"
(verb)   (adjective)   (made-up word)

POOF! Mollie's _____ _____ right
(plural noun)   (verb)

before her eyes. In fact, one by one, everyone's _____
(plural noun)

_____. They were all _____, but _____
(verb)   (adjective)   (adjective)

The wicked _____ was _____ by the
(noun)   (verb)

_____, and everyone _____ happily ever after!
(noun)   (verb)

"Multicolored hand-painted frame" by Milano83 at Freepik.com

26

Story Tell Draw #1

Use the space below to draw Mollie and where she lives, what she finds, and other characters and parts of the story.

Writing Prompt #1

Priscilla's favorite words are adjectives, which describe how nouns look, feel, taste, smell, and sound.

What are your favorite words? What makes them special to you?

_____

_____

_____

_____

_____

_____

_____

_____

Writing Prompt Draw #1

Use the space below to draw pictures of your favorite words.

I am not afraid of storms for I am learning
how to sail my ship.
Louisa May Alcott

Quote Draw #2

Use the space below to draw a picture of yourself on your ship in the middle of a storm.

Word Search #2

The following words can be found in the diagram below, reading forward, backward, up, down, and diagonally. Find the words and circle them.

freeze	scary
funny	wizard
jump	write
cereal	thunder
mushy	squiggly
bewitching	disappear

```
X D T Q B E W I T C H I N G C V
F U I F V B W S C A R Y R W C W
U A V S M M H S S W I Z A R D R
N D E L A J F C V W S U C P N I
N T J U M P S J N X F O U W K T
Y X W F J I P N B B Q F N Z K E
P U G I O J Y E C C Q M P O R D
I O O F K T P T A G Q V W W I W
G Y Q N G F X E Y R I Z U U P I
M M T E Q A I W L L B L F I C A
U F Y Z J B F H S T G N X Q R F
S Q M E A G V M Z L M G H I Y J
H U D E S W E Y V O A A I V S T
Y C E R E A L J Q K B V A U N V
G I I F G U U O D T Y X X R Q T
C P P Q T H U N D E R Q P M I S
```

Scramble #2

Below is list of scramble words. Unscramble all the letters to reveal the words.

1. OWYLSL =

_____

2. GYNDEAREL =

_____

3. ENCIGHIBTW =

_____

4. EFUCARGYLL =

_____

5. DIAWZR =

_____

6. EFEYHART =

_____

7. STUYM =

_____

8. NRSTO =

_____

Cryptogram #2

Each of these Cryptograms is a message in substitution code. THE SILLY DOG might become UJD WQPPZ BVN if U is substituted for T, J for H, D for E, etc. One way to break the code is to look for repeated letters. E, T, A, O, N, R, and I are the most often used letters. A single letter is usually A or I; OF, IS, and IT are common 2-letter words; try THE or AND for a 3-letter group.

The code is different for each Cryptogram. A Scratch Paper page is provided, and each puzzle includes three Hints to help you find the solution.

1. Vn eslehu uppzu vzrwuuvasp yonvs vn vu fwop. (Opsuwo Zeofpse) Hints: N = T U = S P = E

2. Xct mal aw xchw tzy xhbh qzbw lz dliwo zyl? (Ob. Dhydd) Hints: X = W A = I W = N

3. Smoo nvuvi lxkvn, nlmip rj vxytl. (Bmjmivnv jeduvec) Hints: N = S L = T M = A

Scratch Paper

Adverb Sort

Read the list of adverbs in the Word Bank. Then write each word in the correct section below the list.

Remember:

Adverbs describe **when**, **where**, and **how** an action takes place.

Word Bank

above	always	anytime	anywhere
below	carefully	everywhere	gently
happily	heavily	here	loudly
magically	never	nowhere	often
quietly	secretly	sometimes	somewhere
soon	thankfully	there	today
tomorrow	whenever	where	wherever
	wishfully	yesterday	

When

Where

How

While adverbs modify verbs, adjectives, and other adverbs, more often than not they are used to add emphasis to a verb.

The following sentences include adverbs modifying a verb. Read each sentence, underline the verb, then circle the adverb. The first sentence has been completed for you. Hint: One sentence has two verbs with a modifying adverb.

1. Finn <u>runs</u> (faster) than his brother.

2. A cat's howl often sounds like a baby's cry.

3. Freddy may be small, but he yells louder than anyone in class.

4. George swam farther than his sister at the lake.

5. Greta slammed the door forcefully and unfortunately broke the lock.

6. Justine breathed deeply in the garden.

7. Many trees live longer than people.

8. Marshall read the story more carefully than Calvin.

9. Nicholas arrived at school earlier than Jonathan.

10. Noah finished his work quickly.

11. Ophelia jumps higher than Sylvia in gym class.

12. Penelope turned her head slowly.

13. Rachel focused harder on the test than Jill.

14. Rain sometimes makes Brianna sleepy.

15. Ruby sings quieter than Sarah.

Crossword #2

Across

2 Enchanted (7)
6 Like candy or sugar (5)
7 Creepy; frightening (5)
9 Root vegetables that are baked, boiled, or fried (8)
10 On the previous day (9)
12 Food made from dough and baked (5)
13 To repeat a phrase using rhythm (5)
15 Soft and furry (6)
18 To cook by dry heat in an oven or on stones (4)

Down

1 Without speed (6)
3 Spirit of a dead person (5)
4 With thought and awareness (9)
5 Without the knowledge of others (8)
8 Very famous; traditional (9)
11 Without light (4)
12 To cook in bubbling, very hot water (4)
13 To prepare food for eating (4)
14 On this present day (5)
15 To harden into ice by removing heat (6)
16 Hideous; unattractive (4)
17 Small being with a human form and magical powers (5)

Cell Phone Mania #2

The messages below are in a number code based on how text messages are formed on a cell phone. Each number represents one of the letters shown on the picture of the phone to the right. You must decide which letter to use. A number is not necessarily the same letter each time.

1. 86 53276 86 7323 47 86 54448 2 3473.
   (842867 4846)

2. 86329 2 732337, 86667769 2 532337.
   (9. 387735626)

Sentence Mania #2

Priscilla again needs your help. She has a new Word Bank and five new sentences with missing words.

Read the sentences and the list of nouns, verbs, adverbs, and adjectives. Then, using the word clue, select the correct word to fill in each blank. Remember, use each word only once and do not use any of the crossed-out words.

Word Bank

~~cat~~	dog	horse	pig
rhinoceros	pounced	barks	jumped
~~snorts~~	charges	~~quietly~~	~~always~~
~~gracefully~~	boldly	~~wild~~	sometimes
sneaky	~~clumsy~~	proud	~~smelly~~

1. The _____ _cat_ _quietly_ _____ on the mouse.

2. The _clumsy_ _____ _always_ _____ .

3. The _____ _____ _gracefully_ _____ over the fence.

4. The _smelly_ _____ _snorts_ _____ .

5. The _wild_ _____ _____ _____ the zoo's visitors.

How Many Words #2

Using the letters in the word shown below, try to find as many 3-letter, 4-letter, 5-letter, 6-letter, and 7-letter words as you can. Write the words you discover in the spaces provided below. The first word has been provided for you.
NOTE: There are more possible word choices than spaces.

EXTRATERRESTRIAL

art _____   _____

_____   _____

_____   _____

_____   _____

_____   _____

_____   _____

_____   _____

_____   _____

_____   _____

Keywords #2

To solve this puzzle, fill in the blanks below with the correct missing letter and then transfer the letter to the corresponding numbered square in the diagram below. Be careful! The puzzle is not as simple as it may first appear!

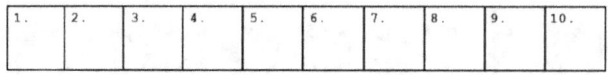

1. c h a _ g e

2. s _ y l y

3. w _ z a r d

4. o f t e _

5. s t _ m p

6. p o u n _ e

7. w r i t _

8. c e _ e a l

9. s n _ w

10. g h o _ t

Two In #2

Place two letters on the dashes to complete a word on the left and to begin another word on the right. For example, **SE** in between PLEA and VEN would completed **PLEASE** and begin **SEVEN**.

1. a c _ _ a d

2. c h _ _ l y

3. d e _ _ b r a r y

4. a d j e c t i _ _ r b

5. a c _ _ a v i l y

Crypto Words #2

Each of these Crypto Words is written in substitution code. SILLY might become WQPPZ if W is substituted for S, Q for I, P for L, etc. When you have identified a word, use the known letters to decode the other words in the list. A Scratch Paper page is provided along with three Hints to help you.

Hints: Q = C K = E A = L

1. TLGHK = _____

2. FLUQKVCAAZ = _____

3. VKUHSKLZ = _____

4. VUAA = _____

5. ONGA = _____

6. QAKUM = _____

7. QSUMH = _____

8. QSULFK = _____

Scratch Paper

Dittos #1

Form 5 different 5-letter words by using all the given letters and adding the letter in the **Free Letter Box** as often as necessary. Cross off each letter in the **Letter Bank** as you use it.

Free Letter	Letter Bank
O	c d e f i l l m n p r r s t t u u u w y

1. ____ ____ ____ ____ ____

2. ____ ____ ____ ____ ____

3. ____ ____ ____ ____ ____

4. ____ ____ ____ ____ ____

5. ____ ____ ____ ____ ____

Story Tell #2

Ready for some more storytelling fun?

The story here includes a new challenge: plural nouns. Remember, "plural" means "more than one."

To form a plural noun, most of the time you add the letter "s" to the end of a single noun: *boy* becomes *boys*, *star* becomes *stars*, *spider* becomes *spiders*, and so on.

But some nouns don't follow this rule: *mouse* changes to *mice*, *goose* changes to *geese*, *child* changes to *children*, etc. To check on the plural form of a noun, use your dictionary.

Remember, the parts that make up a story are:

- ✓ A main character (WHO)
- ✓ A problem (WHAT and WHY)
- ✓ A setting where the story happens (WHERE and WHEN)
- ✓ A solution (HOW)

To create your story, you combine the WHO, WHAT, WHY, WHERE, WHEN, and HOW using the type of word listed.

There are many, many ways to complete the story on the next page. You can be silly or serious, sad or happy, scared or brave.

So, shake up your creative juices, and set your imagination free!

_____, Ezra wants to _____ a _____.
(Adverb)   (verb)   (noun)

The problem is, he doesn't _____ _____.
                                    (verb)   (plural noun)

_____ can Ezra _____ _____?
(Adverb)   (verb)   (plural noun)

He could _____ them, but he doesn't have _____.
            (verb)   (noun)

He could _____ his _____'s _____,
            (verb)   (noun)   (plural noun)

but those _____ are _____.
              (plural noun)   (adjective)

_____, Ezra remembers his _____ has
(Adverb)   (noun)

_____, and they are NOT _____!
(plural noun)   (adjective)

So, Ezra _____ his _____ if he can
            (verb)   (noun)

_____ his _____. His _____
(verb)   (plural noun)   (noun)

_____. _____, Ezra and his _____
(verb)   (Adverb)   (noun)

_____ a _____ _____,
(verb)   (adjective)   (noun)

and Ezra is _____.
                (adjective)

Story Tell Draw #2

Use the space below to draw Ezra, what he needs, what he wants to do, and any other elements from the story.

Writing Prompt #2

Priscilla loves to visit the library to read new books and find new words for her collection.

What is your favorite place to go? What do you do there?

_____

_____

_____

_____

_____

_____

_____

_____

Writing Prompt Draw #2

Use the space below to draw a picture of your favorite place, and what makes it special to you.

Try to be a rainbow in someone's cloud.
Maya Angelou

Quote Draw #3

Use the space below to draw a picture of yourself with your own rainbow.

Word Search #3

The following words can be found in the diagram below, reading forward, backward, up, down, and diagonally. Find the words and circle them.

charge
usually
growl
icecream
magical
wild

library
ghost
clean
snow
scary
goofy

```
V U E M Z J P I C E C R E A M G
W L S L Z L O S C A R Y I A S S
I A C U G O O F Y V K B Q H X R
L I V E A G M I B R V A A L H M
D G R O W L W H Y L P Y D H Z G
D J I T R F L L Z A P F N Y H F
T I G E P S B Y W Q N L P R T O
X W Y F Q P L B P M R V A P C F
J L M O B F Q Y V D K L U D Z S
A Y E Y Q N J R D Y W I Y W B
S C G H M O W O T M R M P Q W A
N K R A A D A Y C L E A N B Q M
O L A I P H Q N D P O G R X B U
W G H O S T T Q N G C C W B Z D
H Z C D K A C L Q O X Y E E I P
S I E H O B I M A G I C A L J L
```

Scramble #3

Below is list of scramble words. Unscramble all the letters to reveal the words.

1. UPJM = _____

2. OUYLDL = _____

3. ESLWEYT = _____

4. OFNET = _____

5. RNRHICSOOE = _____

6. TSUMY = _____

7. LIPNA = _____

8. GRTUN = _____

Cryptogram #3

Each of these Cryptograms is a message in substitution code. THE SILLY DOG might become UJD WQPPZ BVN if U is substituted for T, J for H, D for E, etc. One way to break the code is to look for repeated letters. E, T, A, O, N, R, and I are the most often used letters. A single letter is usually A or I; OF, IS, and IT are common 2-letter words; try THE or AND for a 3-letter group.

The code is different for each Cryptogram. A Scratch Paper page is provided, and each puzzle includes three Hints to help you find the solution.

1. Ped vdmp pexjzm xj kxod whdj'p
   pexjzm; peda'hd asch ohxdjtm.
   (Wjsjanscm)   Hints: **P = T J = N D = E**

2. Iwf geri houuokbqi iwodl paebi
   scoiodl or scoiodl iwf uocri qodf.
   (Pgoi Jpqpdico)   Hints: **C = R E = O I = T**

3. C wqty drfdpb yfn innwb ca lp
   tnuwqy; naq yn oqdh, naq yn focyq
   ca. (Oniqoy Rnvcb Byqeqabna)
                              Hints: **Y = T N = O A = N**

56

Scratch Paper

Parts of Speech Sort

Read the list of words in the Word Bank. Then write each word in the correct section below the list.

Remember:

Nouns name people, places and things.
Verbs show action or state of being.
Adjectives describe how nouns feel, taste, smell, sound, and look.

Word Bank

bark	cat	disappear	clumsy	dog	horse
jump	pig	pounce	proud	smelly	sneaky
snort	gorilla	wild	gloat	tornado	fling
cereal	goofy	peculiar	dinosaur	charge	mushy
noisy	growl	airplane	lumpy	rise	wren

Nouns	Verbs	Adjectives

Sometimes, words can be a noun in one sentence, a verb in another sentence, and an adjective in yet another sentence! While this can be confusing, using context clues can help you determine which part of speech the word represents.

The following sentence groups use an underlined word in three different ways. Read each sentence, then in the space provided, write whether the underlined word is an adjective, a noun, or a verb. The first sentence has been completed for you.

1. Geoffrey put his dirty clothes in the wash.   noun

2. Geoffrey's mom said he couldn't play until he washed his laundry.

3. He also had to put away his washed clothes.

4. Last week, a new restaurant opened downtown.

5. An open door greeted new customers with a musical tone when they walked inside.

6. The restaurant's opening was quite a success.

7. There is a dance at the school tonight.

8. Gloria has a dance recital next week.

9. Babies are so adorable when they dance.

10. Watch your step; the stairs are slippery.

11. If you step in the puddle, you will get pants wet.

12. Jonah uses a step stool to reach the top shelf in his closet.

Crossword #3

Across

2 Not dirty or cluttered (5)
7 Mixture of water and ice seen in the sky (5)
9 Wavy and twisting (8)
10 Extremely large; enormous (4)
13 Fuzzy, light, and downy (8)
14 To make a deep, heavy sound, like thunder (6)
15 With no sound or speech (8)
17 Dangerous windstorm; also called a twister (7)
18 Distant (7)
19 Noise heard during storms (7)
20 Comical; humorous (5)
21 To vanish or become invisible (9)
22 Most of the time (5)
24 To utter a deep sound with anger (5)

Down

1 Splendid in appearance (11)
3 In a noisy manner (6)
4 Moving in a snakelike or wormlike manner (6)
5 Ice crystals falling from clouds (4)
6 Many times (7)
8 Extinct land animals from the distant past (8)
10 To visit or appear regularly, like a ghost (5)
11 Ape from the forests of central West Africa (7)
12 Behaving kindly and without violence (6)
15 In a smooth and agreeable manner (6)
16 Playful elf from Irish folk tales (10)
18 To hang in the air (5)
23 To drop down suddenly (4)

Cell Phone Mania #3

The messages below are in a number code based on how text messages are formed on a cell phone. Each number represents one of the letters shown on the picture of the phone to the right. You must decide which letter to use. A number is not necessarily the same letter each time.

1. 843 72274378 666368 47 259297 5878
   233673 968 78278. (7837436 5464)

2. 968 6878 23 843 242643 968 9474 86
   733 46 843 96753. (6242862 426344)

Sentence Mania #3

Priscilla is at it again. She has another new Word Bank, and six more sentences with missing words.

Read the sentences and the new list of nouns, verbs, adverbs, and adjectives. Then, using the word clue, select the correct word to fill in each blank to complete the sentences. As before, use each word only once and do not use any of the crossed-out words.

Word Bank

wizard	ghost	fairy	leprechauns	clouds	thunder
chanted	float	~~haunts~~	disappear	~~twinkles~~	~~rumbled~~
~~gently~~	~~often~~	~~secretly~~	usually	silently	loudly
~~magical~~	tiny	scary	~~legendary~~	~~fluffy~~	faraway

1. The <u>magical</u> _____ <u>secretly</u> _____.

2. The _____ _____ <u>often twinkles.</u>

3. The _____ _____ _____ <u>haunts</u> the graveyard.

4. The <u>fluffy</u> _____ <u>gently</u> _____ across the sky.

5. The <u>legendary</u> _____ _____ _____ before they can be caught.

How Many Words #3

Using the letters in the word shown below, try to find as many 3-letter, 4-letter, 5-letter, 6-letter, and 7-letter words as you can. Write the words you discover in the spaces provided below. The first word has been provided for you.
NOTE: There are more possible word choices than spaces.

FLABBERGASTED

area _____   _____

_____   _____

_____   _____

_____   _____

_____   _____

_____   _____

_____   _____

_____   _____

Keywords #3

To solve this puzzle, fill in the blanks below with the correct missing letter and then transfer the letter to the corresponding numbered square in the diagram below. Be careful! The puzzle is not as simple as it may first appear!

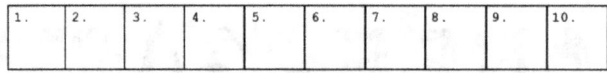

1. h u _ e

2. s c a _ y

3. c h _ r g e

4. _ h a n t

5. g _ n t l y

6. s o _ t l y

7. l _ m p y

8. a _ w a y s

9. w i _ d

10. s h _ l y

Two In #3

Place two letters on the dashes to complete a word on the left and to begin another word on the right. For example, **SE** in between **PLEA** and **VEN** would completed **PLEASE** and begin **SEVEN**.

1. m a g i c _ _ r e a d y

2. c h _ _ e c r e a m

3. g o _ _ t e n

4. b a _ _ u n d e r

5. c e r e _ _ w a y s

Crypto Words #3

Each of these Crypto Words is written in substitution code. SILLY might become WQPPZ if W is substituted for S, Q for I, P for L, etc. When you have identified a word, use the known letters to decode the other words in the list. A Scratch Paper page is provided along with three Hints to help you.

Hints: S = D R = Y V = U

1. UWLHB = _____

2. IVJXHR = _____

3. QJGGR = _____

4. IWTGB = _____

5. HJSSAGVR = _____

6. UCJGB = _____

7. VJXZR = _____

8. SFHTZZATC = _____

Scratch Paper

Interweave #2

Rearrange and distribute the four letters accompanying each row so that you form a larger common word.

1. i s l e : __ __ __ __ n t l y

2. a c r e : i __ __ c __ e __ m

3. a r t y : f e __ __ h e __ __

4. b e n t : __ __ w i __ c h i __ g

5. d e n y : s u __ d __ __ l __

Story Tell #3

Now that you have completed two Story Tells, it's time to stretch your imagination further with another fill-in-the-blank story, one where you practice using context clues.

Context clues are hints to help you understand meaning. They are especially helpful when there are difficult words or phrases in a sentence.

They are also helpful when trying to complete a fill-in-the-blank story.

There are five main types of context clues:

- ✓ Definition – explanation follows the word or phrase
- ✓ Restatement – word or phrase is rewritten in a simpler way
- ✓ Contrast – signal word is used with the opposite meaning
- ✓ Punctuation – use of quotation marks, dashes, parentheses or brackets, or italics to provide definition
- ✓ Roundabout – clues are found in sentences before or after

The key to figuring out context clues for a fill-in-the-blank story is to read the sentences carefully. How do they fit together? Is there more than one character? Do the characters talk? Are there signal words, such as "but," "like," "also," or "so"?

But, though there are context clues to help you create your story, there are many ways to make your ideas fit the sentences. So, on your mark, get set... and GO! And as always, have fun.

One day, a _____ arrived in town. He _____ a _____
　　　　　　　(noun)　　　　　　　　　　　　　　　　　(verb)　　　　　　　(noun)
and a backpack. He tried to _____, but everyone covered their
　　　　　　　　　　　　　　　　　　(verb)
_____ and ran _____. They were _____. So, the
　　(noun)　　　　　　　　　　(adverb)　　　　　　　　　　(adjective)
_____ went to the _____ instead.
　　(noun)　　　　　　　　　　　(noun)
In the _____, the _____ tried to _____ to the
　　　　(noun)　　　　　　　　　　(noun)　　　　　　　　　(verb)
_____. They didn't run, but still seemed to be _____.
　(plural noun)　　　　　　　　　　　　　　　　　　　　　　　　(adjective)

"Why are you _____?" the _____ asked the _____.
　　　　　　　　(adjective)　　　　　　　　(noun)　　　　　　　　　(plural noun)
The _____ said, "It's because your _____ are _____."
　　　(noun)　　　　　　　　　　　　　　　　　(plural noun)　　　　(adjective)
The _____ said, "It's because your _____ is _____."
　　　(noun)　　　　　　　　　　　　　　　　　(noun)　　　　　　(adjective)
And the _____ said, "It's because your _____ have _____."
　　　　(noun)　　　　　　　　　　　　　　　　(plural noun)　　　(plural noun)
The _____ nodded. "I need a _____, a _____, and a
　　　(noun)　　　　　　　　　　　　　　(noun)　　　　　　　(noun)
_____ so I don't look _____."
　　(noun)　　　　　　　　　　　(adjective)

After he _____, the _____ shared _____ and
　　　　　(verb)　　　　　　　　(noun)　　　　　　　　(noun)
_____. He _____ had new _____, and he
　　(noun)　　　　　　(adverb)　　　　　　　(plural noun)
was _____.
　　(adjective)

Story Tell Draw #3

Use the space below to draw your main character, the settings, and any other elements and characters from the story.

Writing Prompt #3

Priscilla didn't know how to be a friend, so she never used the words she collected. Then she met Mrs. Thornblossom, who helped share her words instead of just writing them in notebooks.

Write about your best friend. What do you do together? How do you help each other?

_____

_____

_____

_____

_____

_____

_____

Writing Prompt Draw #3

Use the space below to draw a picture of yourself with your best friend.

You must be the change you wish to
see in the world.
Mahatma Gandhi

Quote Draw #4

Use the space below to draw a picture of people helping other people.

Word Search #4

The following words can be found in the diagram below, reading forward, backward, up, down, and diagonally. Find the words and circle them.

chant	today
cat	faraway
stomp	usually
float	fairy
wild	magical
plain	library

F Q S L W Z S Y V L D N H I M L

Y L M B X S U E Q K Q F P P I L

A T B N X W S O P E K L O B W A

W O J K I M X P V K B O R H M C

A D Z Z G E Q R U G G A W T E I

R A F S M S H Q D W R T N M H G

A Y A V Z F L U P Y N C B M C A

F I I Q S Z L Y G H S K A E D M

I V R G E I Y S M E R R P M H D

O J Y P R L R F J R R I X Y B I

Y G L T L H B R M J K Y P O C Q

E O X A H D H W V Y C F L Q U O

N S U C P V R V G Y T N A H C W

Y S K G I J U L Z Y A X I G D E

U C Z D F E T Z S H S H N C J D

J S T O M P I A I T W I L D G R

Scramble #4

Below is list of scramble words. Unscramble all the letters to reveal the words.

1. YDULSEND =
   _____

2. NYUNF =
   _____

3. LIWD =
   _____

4. YFARETEH =
   _____

5. NACHT =
   _____

6. TODRANO =
   _____

7. GECHRA =
   _____

8. UYMLP =
   _____

Cryptogram #4

Each of these Cryptograms is a message in substitution code. THE SILLY DOG might become UJD WQPPZ BVN if U is substituted for T, J for H, D for E, etc. One way to break the code is to look for repeated letters. E, T, A, O, N, R, and I are the most often used letters. A single letter is usually A or I; OF, IS, and IT are common 2-letter words; try THE or AND for a 3-letter group.

The code is different for each Cryptogram. A Scratch Paper page is provided, and each puzzle includes three Hints to help you find the solution.

1. Dyx cxnd fhaara hn js rpo lahxso.
   (Uxraux Yxacxad)   Hints: A = R H = I X = E

2. Ox dxrc wg ixoa nwep axxc yxflrou.
   (Etdqwgp ldxjzdm)   Hints: X = O O = N A = G

3. Iqq jslo uokigr aie asgk wolk zd jsl
   fitk wfk asloink ws clorlk wfkg.
   (Yiqw Uzrekj)   Hints: Q = L K = E A = C

Scratch Paper

Word Maze

Help Priscilla find the correct path to the Library.

Start here

Now, on the next page, write the word for each picture in the maze in the Noun Chart. Then, write a related verb and adjective for each noun in the charts provided. The first word has been done for you.

Related Verbs	Noun Pictures	Related Adjectives
read	library	quiet
_____	_____	_____
_____	_____	_____
_____	_____	_____
_____	_____	_____
_____	_____	_____
_____	_____	_____
_____	_____	_____
_____	_____	_____
_____	_____	_____

Lastly, use your word list to create at least five different sentences. NOTE: Don't forget to add the correct punctuation.

1. _____
   _____
2. _____
   _____
3. _____
   _____
4. _____
   _____
5. _____
   _____

Crossword #4

Across

1 In a bashful or timid manner (5)
2 Gloomy (5)
3 To utter words or sounds with music (4)
5 To bring the foot down on the ground with force (5)
8 Word that names a person, place, or thing (4)
9 Charming (10)
10 Having a dreamlike and fantastic appearance (16)
13 Shoes with bendable rubber soles (8)
15 Get up from a lying or sitting position (4)
17 With great weight or pressure (7)
18 Without warning (8)
19 Silly and wacky (5)

Down

1 Causing intense interest or emotion (11)
2 Covered with or smelling of mold (5)
4 Word that describes a noun (9)
6 Land that stands high above the ground (8)
7 To utter a deep sound like an ape (5)
11 With a pleasing taste, smell, or sound (7)
12 Happened prior to current time (7)
14 Word that describes a verb (6)
16 Move around in a twisting motion (5)

Cell Phone Mania #4

The messages below are in a number code based on how text messages are formed on a cell phone. Each number represents one of the letters shown on the picture of the phone to the right. You must decide which letter to use. A number is not necessarily the same letter each time.

1. 6623 968 53276 86 7323, 968 9455 23
   3673837 3733. (373337425 36845277)

2. 66 228 63 54636377, 66 628837 469
   76255, 47 3837 927833. (23767'7
   322537)

Sentence Mania #4

Mrs. Thornblossom has made another Word Bank. Priscilla must study for a spelling test, so this time, she needs you to create six sentences on your own.

Choose one word from each section, then combine your choices with other words to make your sentences special. Use each list word once.

✓Remember:

- Every sentence begins with a capital letter; ends with a period, question mark, or exclamation point; and has a subject and a predicate. The predicate is also called a verb.

- The subject is the person, place, or thing the sentence is about.

- The predicate (or verb) tells what the subject is or does.

Word Bank

Nouns

mountain	tornado	gorilla
dinosaur	sneakers	snow

Verbs

fall	swirl	grunt
stomp	drop	rise

Adverbs

darkly	suddenly
heavily	majestically
softly	shyly

Adjectives

squeaky	feathery
huge	magnificent
murky	monstrous

1. _____
   _____

2. _____
   _____

3. _____
   _____

4. _____
   _____

5. _____
   _____

6. _____
   _____

How Many Words #4

Using the letters in the word shown below, try to find as many 3-letter, 4-letter, 5-letter, 6-letter, and 7-letter words as you can. Write the words you discover in the spaces provided below. The first word has been provided for you.
NOTE: There are more possible word choices than spaces.

PHANTASMAGORICAL

pants

Keywords #4

To solve this puzzle, fill in the blanks below with the correct missing letter and then transfer the letter to the corresponding numbered square in the diagram below. Be careful! The puzzle is not as simple as it may first appear!

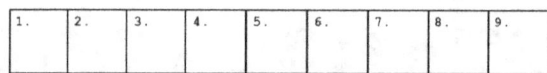

1. _ n e a k y

2. c _ o k

3. c l u _ s y

4. o f t _ n

5. w r i _ e

6. w _ g g l y

7. s _ e l l y

8. h o r s _

9. _ w e e t

Two In #4

Place two letters on the dashes to complete a word on the left and to begin another word on the right. For example, **SE** in between PLEA and VEN would completed **PLEASE** and begin **SEVEN**.

1. g h o _ _ o m p

2. h i _ _ o s t

3. k i _ _ z a r d

4. t o _ _ n n y

5. a m _ _ u n t a i n

Crypto Words #4

Each of these Crypto Words is written in substitution code. SILLY might become WQPPZ if W is substituted for S, Q for I, P for L, etc. When you have identified a word, use the known letters to decode the other words in the list. A Scratch Paper page is provided along with three Hints to help you.

Hints: J = L N = R Q = Y

1. GHNBYFJJQ = _____

2. XNZWB = _____

3. LVCEW = _____

4. MJHZS = _____

5. UBNT = _____

6. EBGNBWJQ = _____

7. GVHSW = _____

8. EVQJQ = _____

Scratch Paper

Dittos #2

Form 5 different 5-letter words by using all the given letters and adding the letter in the Free Letter Box as often as necessary. Cross off each letter in the Letter Bank as you use it.

Free Letter	Letter Bank
e	a a a b d f h i l l n o o p r r s s t t w

1. ___ ___ ___ ___ ___

2. ___ ___ ___ ___ ___

3. ___ ___ ___ ___ ___

4. ___ ___ ___ ___ ___

5. ___ ___ ___ ___ ___

Story Tell #4

Your final fill-in-the-blank story allows you to stretch your imagination even further as you create your own monster tale. The story outline not only asks you to insert nouns, verbs, adjectives, and adverbs, but also, sometimes asks you to provide a specific type of noun, verb, adjective, or adverb, such as a place, a proper  name, or noun group; verbs ending in -ed or -ing; color; or an adverb expressing where or when.

And, as with Story Tell #3, you will continue to practice using context clues. Remember, context clues are hints to help you understand meaning.

There are five main types of context clues:

- ✓ **Definition** – explanation follows the word or phrase
- ✓ **Restatement** – word or phrase is rewritten in a simpler way
- ✓ **Contrast** – signal word is used with the opposite meaning
- ✓ **Punctuation** – use of quotation marks, dashes, parentheses or brackets, or italics to provide definition
- ✓ **Roundabout** – clues are found in sentences before or after

But, while there are context clues to help you create your story, there are many, many ways to make your ideas fit the sentences. So, on your mark, get set...GO! And as always, have fun writing!

A Monstrous Day

It all began when the _____ _____
(adjective)   (noun: type of building)

downtown exploded. Everywhere we looked, the _____ and
(plural noun)

_____ _____ were _____ . The
(adjective: color)   (plural noun)   (verb-ing)

_____ did their best to _____ the _____, but
(noun group)   (action verb)   (noun: place)

only _____ it _____ _____.
(action verb)   (adverb)   (adjective)

Soon after, we _____ a _____ _____
(verb)   (adverb)   (adjective: color)

monster _____ along _____ Street. The
(noun group)   (noun: proper name)

_____ did not _____ what to _____, so
(verb-ing)   (verb)   (verb)

they _____ the monster to keep _____. But the
(verb)   (verb-ing)

monster _____ the _____ and _____
(verb-ed)   (noun group)   (verb-ed)

everything in its way, including _____ and _____
(plural noun)   (plural noun)

Nobody could stop the _____ .
(noun)

So, the _____ _____ to _____ it
(noun group)   (verb-ed)   (verb)

_____ else. However, the _____ _____
(adverb)   (noun)   (verb-ed)

the _____ and _____ _____ away to
(noun group)   (verb-ed)   (adverb)

_____ .
(noun: place)

We were _____ _____ to see it _____.
(adverb)   (adjective)   (verb)

92

Story Tell Draw #4

Use the space below to draw your main character, the monster, settings, and any other elements and characters from the story.

Writing Prompt #4

In Dr. Seuss's book, *Happy Birthday to You!* (1959), the narrator says, "Today you are you! That is truer than true! There is no one alive who is you-er than you!"

Describe yourself, not what you look like, but what makes you different from others. What makes you, YOU?

_____

_____

_____

_____

_____

_____

_____

_____

Writing Prompt Draw #4

Use the space below to draw a picture of yourself doing what makes you extra-special.

"After nourishment, shelter, and companionship, stories are the thing we need most in the world."
Phillip Pullman

Blank Writing Pages

Use the following pages to write your own ideas, including your favorite nouns, verbs, adverbs, and adjectives. Or you might like to expand your responses to the Writing Prompts, add to one or more of the Story Tells, or combine the prompts and the tells to create something new. Just set your imagination free and *write.*

Answer Keys

Note:

Given the various responses possible, there are no Answer Keys for How Many Words, Quotes, Writing Prompts, or Story Tells.

BUMBLEMEYER PUBLICATIONS

Puzzles

Word Search #1 (p. 10)

```
Z X D V U X E N K S X F G N H I
U H C J V L U X D S I B S O E K
X V O J F Y E Z V I B N F E B K
L H O X T B F D X R A Y C V U Q
S G K E W J U C K P K R Q W O U
Q H W J D J P F U B X M S V O Y
R O Y M P X I K N X M G X G N O
I S W D L K Y M H U C R J H Y
C T L L M U E R I C F V R C L
O D C Q E Q I O K V C S Y O T
M D X W X Z N H G Z S A D Z E
I J F M F F E X I D I A Z Y I
I N U V O E Q N D O F R A B O U
R Z P V G O O G I S O Q Y T Q
M V V C D X C C E L A R R E G O
S X S E T X J H L P I G M M C N
```

Scramble #1 (p. 11)

1. AYARFAA = FARAWAY
2. YDTSU – DUSTY
3. AENLC – CLEAN
4. OAEPSTOT – POTATOES
5. DONLSDYE – SUDDENLY
6. NHBGCWIETI – BEWITCHING
7. SYMLLE – SMELLY
8. ISSEMEOMT – SOMETIMES

Cryptogram #1 (p. 12)

1. Wnf vsb isap sbwechbz qw oxhehbz.
   (V.U. Gpohu)
   You can make anything by writing.
   (C. S. Lewis)

2. Mn etdm etnzr pv ctnzbl. (Mddctdm
   Masldu)
   We grow great by dreams.
   (Woodrow Wilson)

3. Inmt tnhy gnv vbzw infptwadtht.
   (Ubyc Xbbgtc)
   Make each day your
   masterpiece. (John Wooden)

Cell Phone Mania #1 (p. 17)

843 8463 47 259297 74448 86 36 9428
47 74448. (627846 588437 5464, 57.)

The time is always right to do what is
right. (Martin Luther King, Jr.)

93 5669 9428 93 273 288 668 9428 93
629 232663. (9455426 74253773273)

We know what we are but not what we
may become. (William Shakespeare)

Crossword #1 (p. 16)

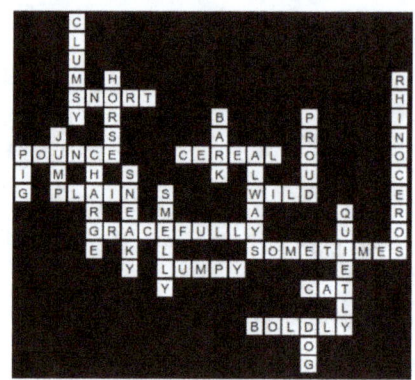

Keywords #1 (p. 20)

feathery

1. often
2. clean
3. bark
4. stomp
5. mushy
6. verb
7. rumble
8. gently

114

Two In #1 (p. 21)

1. ri**se**cretly

2. au**to**day

3. bre**ad**verb

4. re**ad**jective

5. rumb**le**gendary

Interweave #1 (p. 22)

1. aced: **ad** j **ec** t i v e

2. sing: p h a n t a **s** m a **g** o r i c

3. cert: s **e c r t** l y

4. aide: **d i** s a p p **e** a r

5. ache: l **e** p r e **c h a** u n

Scramble #2 (p. 33)

1. OWYLSL – SLOWLY

2. GYNDEAREL – LEGENDARY

3. ENCIGHIBTW – BEWITCHING

4. EFUCARGYLL – GRACEFULLY

5. DIAWZR – WIZARD

6. EFZYHAET – FEATHERY

7. STUYM – MUSTY

8. NRSTO – SNORT

Crypto Words #1 (p. 22)

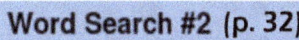

1. QLUURW = WIGGLY

2. YFRYYW = FLUFFY

3. YILBW = FAIRY

4. HSXQ = SNOW

5. UXGZFW = GENTLY

6. KYZXS = OFTEN

7. HGXIVW = SNEAKY

8. UBIDXYRFW = GRACEFULLY

Word Search #2 (p. 32)

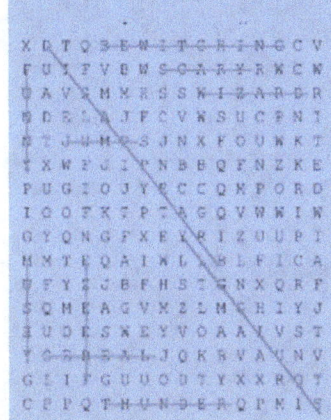

Cryptogram #2 (p. 34)

1. Vn eslehu uppzu vzrwuuvasp yonvs vn vu fwop. (Opsuwo Zeofpse)

   It always seems impossible until it is done. (Nelson Mandela)

2. Xct mal aw xchw tzy xhbh qzbw lz dliwo zyl? (Ob. Dhydd)

   Why fit in when you were born to stand out? (Dr. Seuss)

3. Smoo nvuvi lxkvn, nlmip rj vxytl. (Bmjmivnv jeduvec)

   Fall seven times, stand up eight. (Japanese proverb)

Crossword #2 (p. 38)

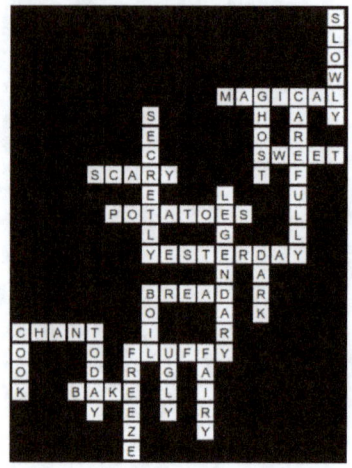

Keywords #2 (p. 42)

r h i n o c e r o s

1. charge
2. shyly
3. wizard
4. often
5. stomp
6. pounce
7. write
8. cereal
9. snow
10. ghost

Dittos #1 (p. 46)

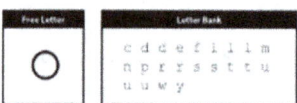

Free Letter	Letter Bank
O	c d d e f l l m n p r r s s t t u u u w y

1. c l o u d
2. p r o u d
3. o f t e n
4. m u s t y
5. s w i r l

Cell Phone Mania #2 (p. 39)

86 53276 7323 47 86 54448 2 3473.
(842867 4846)
To learn to read is to light a fire. (Victor Hugo)

86329 2 732337, 86667769 2 532337.
(9. 387735626)
Today a reader, tomorrow a leader. (W. Fusselman)

Two In #2 (p. 43)

1. a c **re** a d

2. c h **u g** l y

3. d e **li** b r a r y

4. a d j e c t i **ve** r b

5. a c **he** a v i l y

Crypto Words #2 (p. 44)

1.	TLGHK =	WRITE
2.	FLUQKVCAAZ =	GRACEFULLY
3.	VKUHGKLZ =	FEATHERY
4.	VUAA =	FALL
5.	ONGA =	BOIL
6.	QAKUN =	CLEAN
7.	QSUMH =	CHANT
8.	QSULTK =	CHARGE

Word Search #3 (p. 54)

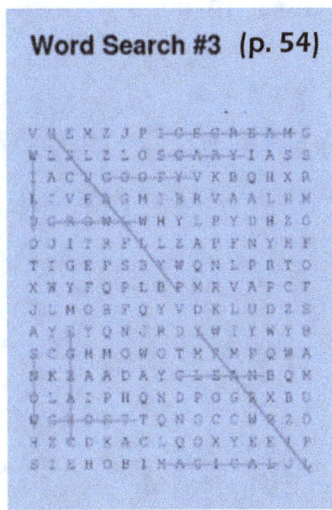

Scramble #3 (p. 55)

1. UPJM = JUMP
2. OUYLDL = LOUDLY
3. ESLWEYT = SWEETLY
4. OFNET = OFTEN
5. RNRHICSOOE = RHINOCEROS
6. TSUMY = MUSTY
7. LIPNA = PLAIN
8. GRTUN = GRUNT

Cryptogram #3 (p. 56)

1. Ped vdmp pexjzm xj kxod whdj'p
   pexjzm; peda'hd asch ohxdjtm.
   (Wisjanscm)

   The best things in life aren't things; they're your
   friends. (Anonymous)

2. Iwf geri houuokbqi iwodl paebi
   scoiodl or scoiodl iwf uocri qodf.
   (Pgoi Jpqpdico)

   The most difficult thing about writing is writing the
   first line. (Amit Kalantri)

3. C wqty drfdpb yfn innwb ca lp
   tnuwqy; naq yn oqdh, naq yn focyq
   ca. (Onigov Rnvcb Bygegabna)

   I kept always two books in my pocket; one to read,
   one to write in. (Robert Louis Stevenson)

Crossword #3 (p. 60)

Cell Phone Mania #3   (p. 61)

843 72274378 666368 47 259297 5878
233673 968 78278. (7837436 5464)
The scariest moment is always just before you start.
(Stephen King)

968 6878 23 843 242643 968 9474 86
733 46 843 96753. (6242862 426344)
You must be the change you wish to see in the world.
(Mahatma Gandhi)

Keywords #3   (p. 64)

g r a c e f u l l y

1. huge
2. scary
3. charge
4. chant
5. gently
6. softly
7. lumpy
8. always
9. wild
10. shyly

117

Two In #3   (p. 65)

1. m a g i c **a l** r e a d y

2. c h **i c** e c r e a m

3. g o **o f** t e n

4. b a **t h** u n d e r

5. c e r e **a l** w a y s

Interweave #2   (p. 68)

1. isle: **s i l e** n t l y

2. acre: i **c e** c r e a m

3. arty: f e **a t** h e **r y**

4. bent: **b e** w i t c h i n **g**

5. deny: s u **d** d e **n** l **y**

Scramble #4   (p. 77)

1. YDULSEND = SUDDENLY

2. NYUNF = FUNNY

3. IWD = WILD

4. YEARETSH = FEATHERY

5. NACHT = CHANT

6. TODRANO = TORNADO

7. GECHRA = CHARGE

8. UYMLP = LUMPY

Crypto Words #3   (p. 66)

1. OWLHB = GHOST

2. IVUXHR = CLUMSY

3. QJGGR = FUNNY

4. IWTGB = CHANT

5. HJSSAGVR = SUDDENLY

6. OGUGR = GRUNT

7. VTXZR = LUMPY

8. SFRTZZATO = DISAPPEAR

Word Search #4   (p. 76)

Cryptogram #4   (p. 78)

1. Dyx cxnd fhaara hn js rpo lahxso.
   (Uxraux Yxacxad)

   The best mirror is an old friend. (George Herbert)

2. Ox dxrc wg ixoa nwep axxc yxflrou.
   (Etdqwap ldxizdm)

   No road is long with good company. (Turkish proverb)

3. Iqq jslo uokigr aie asgk wolk zd jsl fitk wfk asloink ws clorlk wfkg.
   (Yiqw Uzrekj)

   All your dreams can come true if you the courage to pursue them. (Walt Disney)

Crossword #4   (p. 82)

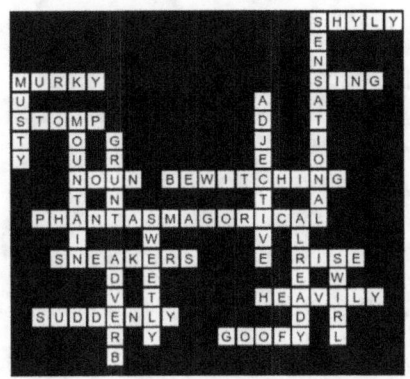

Cell Phone Mania #4   (p. 83)

6623 960 53276 86 7323, 968 9455 23
3673837 3733. (373337425 36845277)

Once you learn to read, you will be forever
free. (Frederick Douglass)

66 228 63 54636377, 66 628837 469
76255, 47 3837 927833. (23767'7
322537)

No act of kindness, no matter how small, is ever
wasted. (Aesop's Fables)

Keywords #4   (p. 86)

s o m e t i m e s

1. s n e a k y
2. c o o k
3. c l u m s y
4. o f t e n
5. w r i t e
6. w i g g l y
7. s m e l l y
8. h o r s e
9. s w e e t

Two In #4   (p. 87)

1. g h o s **t** o m p

2. h i **g h** o s t

3. k i **w i** z a r d

4. t o f **u** n n y

5. a m **m o** u n t a i n

Crypto Words #4   (p. 88)

1. CHNBYFJJQ =   CAREFULLY
2. XNZWB =   WRITE
3. LVCEX =   GHOST
4. MJKZS =   PLAIN
5. UBNT =   VERB
6. EBGNBWJQ =   SECRETLY
7. CVHCX =   CHANT
8. EVQJQ =   SHYLY

Dittos #2   (p. 90)

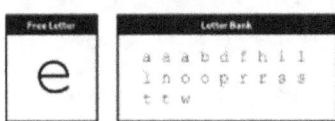

1. p   l   a   i   n
2. h   o   r   s   e
3. f   l   o   a   t
4. b   r   e   a   d
5. s   w   e   e   t

Worksheets

Noun Sort (pp. 14-15)

People	Places	Things
butcher	closet	bread
cashier	house	daffodil
librarian	mountain	potatoes
mail carrier	store	thunder
wizard	school	sneakers
teacher	library	rhinoceros
grandparent	moat	bicycle
aunt	cloud	ostrich
doctor	hospital	jewelry

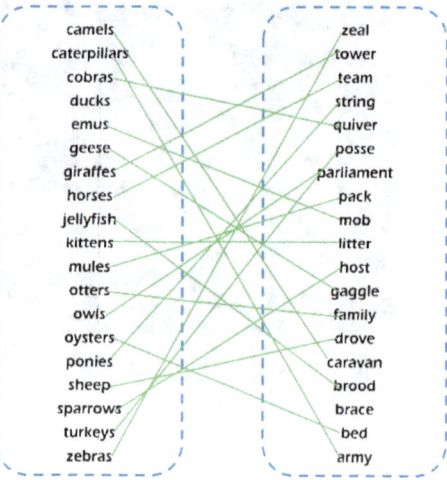

camels
caterpillars
cobras
ducks
emus
geese
giraffes
horses
jellyfish
kittens
mules
otters
owls
oysters
ponies
sheep
sparrows
turkeys
zebras

zeal
tower
team
string
quiver
posse
parliament
pack
mob
litter
host
gaggle
family
drove
caravan
brood
brace
bed
army

Sentence Mania #1 (p. 18)

1. Mrs. Thornblossom carefully _____cooked_____ the lumpy _____cereal_____.

2. The _____plain_____ bread _____slowly_____ bakes in the oven.

3. Priscilla _____boiled_____ mushy _____potatoes_____ for lunch _____today_____.

4. The _____sweet_____ ice cream _____ was frozen _____yesterday_____.

Adverb Sort (pp. 36-37)

When	Where	How
always	here	gently
often	someplace	secretly
sometimes	nowhere	loudly
today	there	quietly
yesterday	everywhere	heavily
never	above	carefully
soon	anywhere	happily
whenever	somewhere	magically
tomorrow	where	thankfully

1. Finn runs faster than his brother.
2. A cat's howl often sounds like a baby's cry.
3. Freddy may be small, but he yells louder than anyone in class.
4. George swam farther than his sister at the lake.
5. Greta slammed the door forcefully and unfortunately broke the lock.
6. Justine breathed deeply in the garden.
7. Many trees live longer than people.
8. Marshall read the story more carefully than Calvin.
9. Nicholas arrived at school earlier than Jonathan.
10. Noah finished his work quickly.
11. Ophelia jumps higher than Sylvia in gym class.
12. Penelope turned her head slowly.
13. Rachel focused harder on the test than Jill.
14. Rain sometimes makes Brianna sleepy.
15. Ruby sings quieter than Sarah.

Sentence Mania #2 (p.40)

1. The _____sneaky_____ cat quietly _____pounced_____ on the mouse.

2. The clumsy _____dog_____ always _____barks_____.

3. The _____proud_____ _____horse_____ gracefully _____jumped_____ over the fence.

4. The smelly _____pig_____ snorts _____boldly_____.

5. The wild _____rhinoceros_____ _____sometimes_____ _____charges_____ the zoo's visitors.

Parts of Speech Sort (pp. 58-59)

Nouns	Verbs	Adjectives
cat	bark	clumsy
dog	charge	proud
horse	jump	smelly
pig	pounce	sneaky
gorilla	snort	wild
tornado	disappear	goofy
cereal	gloat	peculiar
dinosaur	fling	mushy
airplane	growl	noisy
wren	rise	lumpy

1. Geoffrey put his dirty clothes in the <u>wash</u>.   noun

2. Geoffrey's mom said he couldn't play until he <u>washed</u> his laundry.   verb

3. He also had to put away his <u>washed</u> clothes.   adjective

4. Last week, a new restaurant <u>opened</u> downtown.   verb

5. An <u>open</u> door greeted new customers with a musical tone when they walked inside.   adjective

6. The restaurant's <u>opening</u> was quite a success.   noun

7. There is a <u>dance</u> at the school tonight.   noun

8. Gloria has a <u>dance</u> recital next week.   adjective

9. Babies are so adorable when they <u>dance</u>.   verb

10. Watch your <u>step</u>; the stairs are slippery.   noun

11. If you <u>step</u> in the puddle, you will get pants wet.   verb

12. Jonah uses a <u>step</u> stool to reach the top shelf in his closet.   adjective

Sentence Mania #3 (p. 62)

1. The magical _____wizard_____ secretly _____chanted_____.
2. The _____tiny_____ _____fairy_____ often twinkles.
3. The _____scary_____ _____ghost_____ _____usually_____ haunts the graveyard.
4. The fluffy _____clouds_____ gently _____float_____ across the sky.
5. The legendary _____leprechauns_____ _____silently_____ _____disappear_____ before they can be caught.
6. The _____faraway_____ _____thunder_____ rumbled _____loudly_____ during the storm.

Word Maze (pp. 80-81)

NOTE: Related Verbs and Related Adjectives listed are provided for reference only. Your own choices may be different. Also, due to the numerous variations possible, there are no sample sentences given.

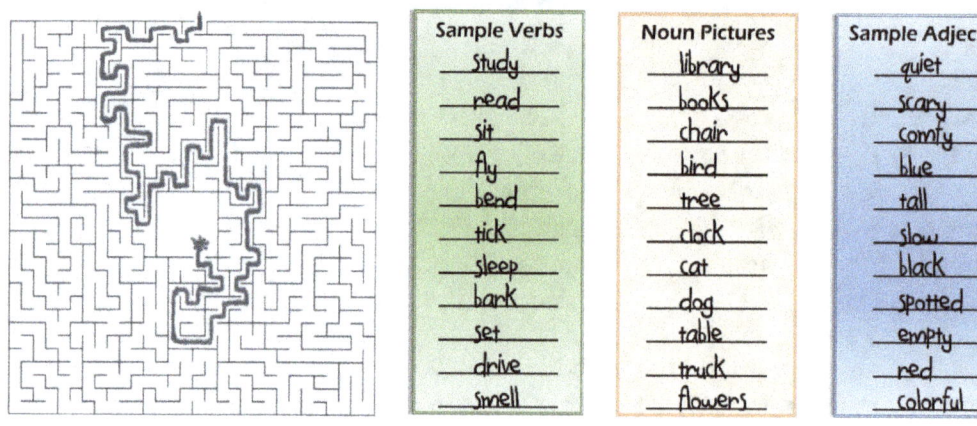

Sample Verbs	Noun Pictures	Sample Adjectives
Study	library	quiet
read	books	scary
sit	chair	comfy
fly	bird	blue
bend	tree	tall
tick	clock	slow
sleep	cat	black
bark	dog	spotted
set	table	empty
drive	truck	red
smell	flowers	colorful

Sentence Mania #4 (p.84)

Sentences will vary. Possible answers include:

1. The magnificent mountain rises majestically above the clouds.
2. The huge gorilla grunted shyly at the crowd.
3. A monstrous dinosaur stomped heavily among the trees.
4. The feathery snow fell softly on the ground.
5. A murky tornado swirled darkly in the distance.
6. My squeaky sneakers suddenly dropped off the shelf.

"There have been great societies that did not use the wheel, but there have been no societies that did not tell stories."

Ursula K. LeGuin

Appendices

Priscilla's Word List (Updated)
More Quotes for Kids
Additional Writing Prompts
Some Excellent Resources

Priscilla's Word List (Updated)

NOUNS	Definition
adjective	word that describes a noun
adverb	word that describes a verb
airplane	powered heavier-than-air aircraft with fixed wings
aunt	the sister of one's father or mother; the wife of one's uncle
bicycle	vehicle with two wheels one behind the other, handlebars, saddle seat, and pedals
bread	food made from dough and baked
broccoli	garden vegetable with thick stem and usually green florets
carrot	garden vegetable with fleshy, green root
cat	feline mammal with whiskers and soft fur
cereal	breakfast food made from grain
cloud	mixture of water and ice seen in the sky
collywobbles	bellyache; intense anxiety in the stomach
daffodil	flower with long, narrow leaves and yellow petals
dinosaur	extinct land animals from the distant past
doctor	person educated and licensed in healing arts; person who has earned the highest academic degree
dog	canine mammal that barks
emu	large, nonflying Australian bird similar but smaller than an ostrich
extraterrestrial	a being from another world
fairy	small being with a human form and magical powers
ghost	spirit of a dead person
gorilla	largest ape from the forests of central West Africa
grandparent	mother or father of one's parent

horse	mammal with hooves that eats hay
ice cream	frozen dessert made from milk and sugar, and mixed with different flavors like vanilla and chocolate
leprechaun	playful elf from Irish folk tales
library	place where books and other reference materials are kept
moat	deep, broad ditch dug around a castle for protection, and usually filled with water
mountain	land mass that stands high above the ground
noun	word that names a person, place, or thing
ostrich	swift-running, nonflying bird of Africa and the Near East
parent	one's mother or father
penguin	flightless bird with webbed feet and paddle-like flippers from the Southern Hemisphere
pig	mammal that snorts and likes mud
potatoes	root vegetable that is baked, boiled, or fried
rhinoceros	huge plant-eating mammal with thick skin and horns
sneakers	shoes with bendable rubber soles
snow	ice crystals falling from clouds
speech	expression of thoughts in spoken words
teacher	one who teaches; an instructor
thunder	booming noise heard during storms
tornado	dangerous windstorm; also called a twister
uncle	the brother of one's mother or father; the husband of one's aunt
verb	word that tells action
wizard	person who practices magic
wren	small songbird with long bill, rounded wings, and short, erect tail

VERBS	Definition
bake	to cook by dry heat in an oven or on stones
bark	to make a loud, sharp cry like a dog
boil	to cook in bubbling, very hot water
bring	to cause to come with oneself; to lead
chant	to repeat a phrase using rhythm
charge	to rush forward as in an attack
cook	to prepare food for eating
disappear	to vanish or become invisible
fall	to drop down suddenly
fling	to throw, especially with force
float	to hang in the air
freeze	to harden into ice by removing heat
gloat	to gaze at or think about something with great satisfaction
grin	to smile broadly; to draw back the lips so as to show the teeth
growl	to utter a deep sound with anger
grumble	to mumble or make unhappy low sounds
grunt	to utter a deep sound like an ape
haunt	to visit or appear regularly, like a ghost
hunt	to pursue for food or sport; to search for
jump	to leap or hop up off a floor or ground
make	to lay out and construct; to bring together
pounce	to swoop down or leap and grab
rise	to get up from a lying or sitting position
rumble	to make a deep, heavy sound, like thunder
scramble	to move or climb with hands and feet
sing	to utter words or sounds with music
snort	to force air through the nostrils
stomp	to bring the foot down on the ground with force
swirl	to move around in a twisting motion
take	to get possession of by skill or force

ADVERBS	Definition
above	at a higher level or layer
absolutely	in a complete manner; a forceful "yes"
already	prior to current time
always	every time
anytime	at any time whatsoever
anywhere	at, in, or to any place or point
below	at a lower level or layer
boldly	without fear or hesitation
carefully	with thought and awareness
clumsily	in an awkward manner or without grace
easily	without difficulty; in an easy manner
everywhere	in or to every place or part
gently	behaving kindly and without violence
gracefully	with elegance and beauty in movement
happily	in a happy manner; with joy
heavily	with great weight or pressure
here	in or at this place
hurriedly	with great speed
later	farther on in time; after the usual time
loudly	in a noisy manner
never	not ever; at no time
now	at the present time or moment
nowhere	not in or at any place
often	many times
quickly	in a quick manner
quietly	without disturbing sound or noise
secretly	without the knowledge of others
shyly	in a bashful or timid manner
silently	with no sound or speech
slowly	without speed
sneakily	in a sly or sneaky manner
softly	in a smooth and agreeable manner
sometimes	now and then
somewhere	in, at, from, or to an unknown place

soon	without much time
suddenly	without warning
sweetly	with a pleasing taste, smell, or sound
thankfully	with thanks or relief
there	in or at that place
today	on this present day
tomorrow	on or for the day after today
tonight	on the present or approaching evening
usually	most of the time; under normal conditions
when	at what time
whenever	at whatever time
where	at, in, or to what place
wherever	anywhere at all
wishfully	with hope
yearly	once per year; every year
yesterday	on the previous day

ADJECTIVES   Definition

bewitching	charming
clean	not dirty or cluttered
clumsy	awkward and without grace
comical	something causing amusement
dark	without light
dusty	filled with or covered by a powder-like layer
fabulous	incredible, astonishing, or exaggerated
faraway	distant
feathery	fuzzy, light, and downy
flabbergasted	feeling intense shock, surprise, or wonder
fluffy	soft and furry
funny	comical; humorous
goofy	silly and wacky
haunted	visited or inhabited by a ghost; bothered or troubled by someone or something
huge	extremely large; enormous

legendary	very famous; traditional
lovely	having qualities that inspire love or admiration
lumpy	chunky; with bumps
magical	enchanted
magnanimous	being generous or forgiving; noble
magnificent	splendid in appearance
marvelous	causing wonder; splendid
murky	gloomy
mushy	squishy and paste-like
musty	covered with or smelling of mold
mystical	having a spiritual meaning or reality
noisy	making noise
nosy	given to prying; inquisitive
pasty	like paste in texture or color
peculiar	different from usual or normal; strange
phantasmagorical	having a dreamlike and fantastic appearance
plain	clear to the eye or ear
proud	honored; satisfied
puffy	soft, light, and fluffy; swollen in size
scary	creepy; frightening
sensational	causing intense interest or emotion
silly	not showing common sense or good judgment; foolish
smelly	having an unpleasant odor
sneaky	sly or tricky
spooky	relating to or resembling ghosts; frightening
squiggly	wavy and twisting
sweet	like candy or sugar
ugly	hideous; unattractive
wiggly	moving in a snakelike or wormlike manner
wild	stormy and untamed

More Quotes for Kids

1. The best things in life aren't things; they're your friends. (Anonymous)

2. You can make anything by writing. (C.S. Lewis)

3. The most difficult thing about writing is writing the first line. (Amit Kalantri)

4. Once you learn to read, you will be forever free. (Frederick Douglass)

5. No road is long with good company. (Turkish proverb)

6. Failure is an event, never a person. (William D. Brown)

7. The time is always right to do what is right. (Martin Luther King, Jr.)

8. We grow great by dreams. (Woodrow Wilson)

9. We know what we are but not what we may become. (William Shakespeare)

10. Fall seven times, stand up eight. (Japanese proverb)

11. Why fit in when you were born to stand out? (Dr. Seuss)

12. It always seems impossible until it is done. (Nelson Mandela)

13. All your dreams can come true if you have the courage to pursue them. (Walt Disney)

14. No act of kindness, no matter how small, is ever wasted. (Aesop Fable)

15. The secret of getting ahead is getting started. (Mark Twain)

Additional Writing Prompts

1. Write about your favorite season of the year. What makes it special to you? What do you like to do at this time of year?

2. You have to decide between a gorilla and a giraffe for a pet. Which one will you choose? Explain your reasons for your choice.

3. If you could choose to be an animal for a day, which animal would you choose to be? Why?

4. Describe something about your bedroom that no one else knows.

5. Imagine you are going to be the first kid to go into outer space. Where will you go? Why do you want to go there? What do you expect to see?

6. Describe what you think would be the best adventure ever.

7. Describe the funniest thing you have ever seen.

8. Write a short story about the strange and crazy noitanimoba you found last night in your bathroom.

9. Describe the most awesome, exciting job you could have.

10. You just found a magic coin. Describe it and then explain what special things it can do. Will you share it with your friends? Why or why not?

11. Tell about the best movie you have ever seen.

12. If you could go anywhere in the world, where would you go? Why?

13. What are three things you like to do when you can't watch television or play video games? What makes these things fun?

14. Describe what you think life will be like when you are 100 years old.

15. What is your favorite food? Why?

Some Excellent Resources

https://school.discoveryeducation.com/

Designed as an education resource in partnership with the Discovery Channel, this website includes a broad range of resources for all disciplines and grade levels. Many offerings—Puzzlemaker, Virtual Field Trips, and several virtual lessons plans—are free.

https://ncte.org/resources

An excellent resource from the National Council of Teachers of English (NCTE) for preschool through college, the website features a ReadWriteThink learning lab with printable and interactive activities. The site also provides links to other web resources, which are updated regularly.

https://www.k12reader.com/grade-level/grades-k-12/

K12Reader provides free reading instruction resources for parents and teachers, with worksheets for spelling, grammar, reading skills, vocabulary, and composition. The Learning Center offers articles and additional online resources for language arts, and there are lesson plan templates, graphic aids, and book lists from key children's literature awards.

Credits and Acknowledgements

Clip art:

https://www.clipartpanda.com/
    page 10: "Happy Kids"; "Star Kids"

https://freedesignfile.com/
    page 32: "Sailing boat marine"

https://all-free-download.com/free-vector/
    page 50: "Hands background" (created by All-free-download)

https://www.jessicaweiblestudios.com/
    pages 50 & 54: "Stick Chicks"; "Stick Dudes" (created by Jessica Weible)

https://www.publicdomainpictures.net/
    page 54: "Rainbow Cloud" (created by X posid)

https://all-free-download.com/free-vector/
    page 76: "Colorful hands" (created by zcool.com.cn)

https://www.freepik.com/
    page 76: "Children together around world" (created by Freepik)

Frames:

https://www.freepik.com/
    page 28: "Multicolored hand-painted frame" (created by Milano83)
    page 72: "Grunge" (created by Kjpargeter)
    page 94: "Grunge frame" (created by vector_corp)

Illustrations:

Interior Priscilla illustrations by Matt Tyree (https://matttyreeart.com/) and copyright © 2013 Evelyn Dunbar Webb

Front and back covers and interior book illustrations, unless otherwise noted above, by MotherWorld, an imprint of Bumblemeyer Publications, copyright © 2024

Meet the Author

A lifelong reader, writer, and logophile, **Evelyn Dunbar Webb** is the recipient of numerous awards for her children's stories, poetry, and essays.

After more than four decades as a mother, business owner, English teacher, and workshop instructor, Evelyn returned to her first love—spinning tales—in 2016. When she is not writing or traveling, she spends her days reading, drawing, or riding her red tricycle.

A native of Connecticut now living in rural central Virginia, Evelyn shares a home with her husband, thousands of books (many of which are hand-me-downs), and the occasional grandchild.

To logophiles everywhere,

I'd love to read what you've created! To share your stories and comments, or ask questions, please feel free to email me through my publisher at bumblemeyerpub2017@outlook.com.

To join my mailing list and learn more about my other products and publications, please visit me at: https://evelyndunbarwebb.com.

You can also follow me on X (formally Twitter) at https://twitter.com/@EDWebbWriter.

And look for Priscilla's return in her second adventure with words, *Priscilla's Prepositions*, coming soon.

Happy word-collecting and sharing!

Evelyn Dunbar Webb
January 2024

www.ingramcontent.com/pod-product-compliance
Lightning Source LLC
Chambersburg PA
CBHW080959120626
46546CB00010B/2963